Look Inside a
Tide Pool

Louise Spilsbury

Heinemann
LIBRARY
Chicago, Illinois

Edited by Rebecca Rissman, Dan Nunn, and John-Paul Wilkins
Designed by Steve Mead
Original illustrations © Capstone Global Library Ltd 2013
Illustrations by Gary Hanna
Picture research by Ruth Blair
Production by Alison Parsons
Originated by Capstone Global Library Ltd
Printed in China

16 15 14 13 12
10 9 8 7 6 5 4 3 2 1

Library of Congress Cataloging-in-Publication Data
Spilsbury, Louise.
  Tide pool / Louise Spilsbury.—1st ed.
    p. cm.—(Look inside)
  Includes bibliographical references and index.
  ISBN 978-1-4329-7197-7 (hb)—ISBN 978-1-4329-7204-2 (pb)
1. Tide pool ecology—Juvenile literature. 2. Microorganisms—
Juvenile literature. 3. Niche (Ecology)—Juvenile literature. I. Title.

QH541.5.S35S745 2013
577.69'9—dc23   2012011821

Acknowledgments

We would like to thank the following for permission to reproduce
photographs: iStockphoto p. 14 (© Amy Riley); Naturepl pp. 7 (©
Ernie Janes), 8 (© Wild Wonders of Europe / Lundgren), 9 (© Gary
K. Smith), 12 (© Philippe Clement), 17 (© Florian Graner), 19 (©
Solvin Zankl), 21 (© Alan James), 23 (© Christophe Courteau),
25 (© Sue Daly), 26 (© Robert Thompson), 28 (© Simon
Colmer); Photoshot p. 27 (© NHPA); Science Photo Library pp.
13 (ALEXANDER SEMENOV), 15 (FRED WINNER/JACANA);
Shutterstock pp. 5 (© Wesley Cowpar), 6 (© Stephen Aaron Rees),
11 (© Martin Fowler), 20 (© nanadou), 24 (© vilainecrevette), 29
(© Juriah Mosin); Superstock p. 18 (© F1 ONLINE).

Cover photograph of starfish resting on a rock with seaweed,
snails, and barnacles in a tide pool on Cape Cod, Massachusetts,
reproduced with permission of iStockphoto (© Amy Riley).

We would like to thank Michael Bright and Diana Bentley for their
invaluable help in the preparation of this book.

Every effort has been made to contact copyright holders of any
material reproduced in this book. Any omissions will be rectified
in subsequent printings if notice is given to the publisher.

Disclaimer

All the Internet addresses (URLs) given in this book were valid at
the time of going to press. However, due to the dynamic nature of
the Internet, some addresses may have changed, or sites may have
changed or ceased to exist since publication. While the author
and publisher regret any inconvenience this may cause readers, no
responsibility for any such changes can be accepted by either the
author or the publisher.

Contents

Some words are shown in bold, **like this**. You can find out what they mean by looking in the glossary.

At the Top

A tide pool is a pond on the **seashore** that fills with seawater. A **habitat** is a place where animals find **shelter** or food. We find some animals at the top of tide pool habitats.

A limpet is a sea snail with a hard, pointed shell. It clings to rocks so that waves do not wash it away. It moves around to eat seaweed that grows on the rocks.

▲ Limpets can often be found in tide pools.

An oystercatcher is a **seabird** with a long, red beak. Oystercatchers fly down to eat animals such as mussels in the tide pools.

▼ Oystercatchers watch tide pools for food.

▲ This oystercatcher is eating a mussel.

Oystercatchers use their strong beaks to push limpets and other shells from the rocks. Sometimes they smash shells on rocks to open them. Then they eat the juicy animals inside.

Shore crabs also come to tide pools to feed. They walk sideways over rocks and seaweed, looking for small or dead animals to eat. They catch their lunch with their big **pincers**!

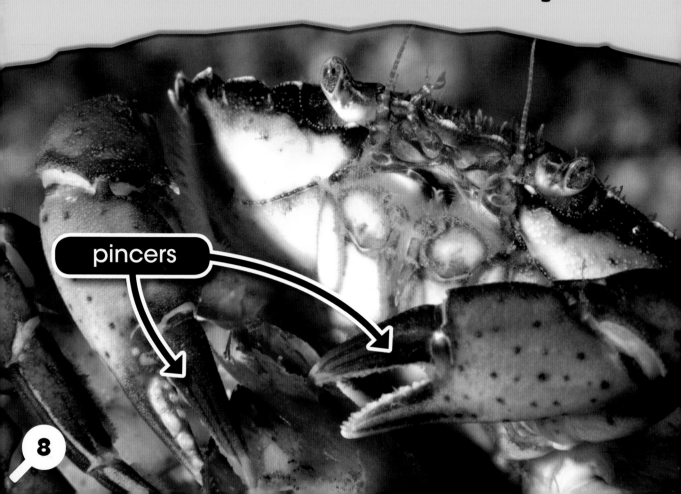

▼ Crab pincers are hard and strong!

pincers

▲ Crabs can be difficult to spot in a tide pool.

Shore crabs are the same color as the rocks and seaweed. This helps the crabs to hide from hungry **seabirds** that try to eat them.

On the Rocks

Some creatures live in tide pools where they stick to one rock and stay there all their lives. Others move around on the rocks looking for food.

Dog whelks hunt limpets and other animals with shells. They use their sharp tongues to drill holes into the shells of their **prey**. Then they suck out and eat the animal inside.

Dog whelks have ▶ small, pointed shells.

11

Mussels have two shells that can close tightly together. They grow and live together in groups on rocks. Each mussel makes sticky threads to fasten itself to rocks.

▼ Mussels close their shells when out of water.

▲ Mussels open their shells when underwater.

Mussels open their shells to eat tiny bits of food floating in the water. They stick out a tube and suck in water. Then they eat the food and spit the water out!

Starfish have five arms with tiny suckers underneath. These suck onto rock and seaweed so that starfish can move around a tide pool and find food.

▼ Starfish can grow a new arm if they lose one.

▲ This starfish has wrapped up a meal!

The starfish uses the suckers on its arms to open shells. It pushes its stomach into the shell and around the animal inside. Then the starfish **digests** its **prey**.

In the Water

Some animals swim around underwater in the tide pool. They may move from pool to pool to find **shelter** or food.

Female lumpfish lay their **eggs** in tide pools. The **male** fish uses a strong sucker on his belly to stick himself to a rock near the eggs. He keeps them safe from starfish and crabs until they **hatch**.

▲ Lumpfish can suck onto a rock!

Prawns have ten legs that help them swim and walk on rocks. The front legs have **pincers** for grabbing food. Prawns eat anything from seaweed to tiny bits of dead animals.

▼ Prawns kick their legs to swim.

▲ Prawns are good at hiding in tide pools.

Prawns are almost see-through. This makes it hard for hungry fish to spot them! Prawns also hide under seaweed to keep out of sight.

A gunnel is a long, thin fish with marks on its back that look a bit like eyes. The marks can fool **predators** into thinking the gunnel is a much bigger fish than it is, so they leave it alone.

▼ Gunnel fish twist and curl to swim.

▲ Gunnels often hide among plants.

The gunnel wriggles like a snake through the water. It swims down to the bottom of the tide pool and looks for worms hidden in the sand to eat.

Rock Bottom

There are some very interesting animals living at the bottom of the tide pool, too.

A sea slug uses the two feelers by its mouth to feel its way around the bottom of the tide pool. It uses the two **antennae** on top of its head to smell out food to eat.

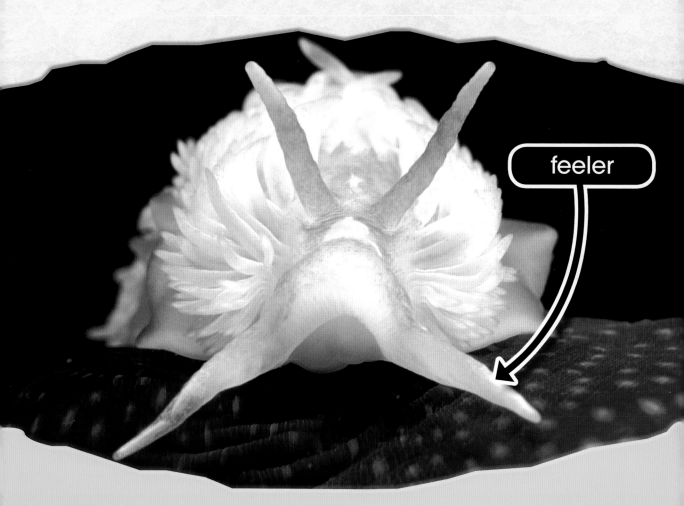

feeler

▲ Sea slugs often eat sea anemones.

Sea anemones look like strange flowers stuck to rocks, but they are animals. They wave their long **tentacles** around to catch food from the water.

▼ Sea anemones are meat-eating animals.

tentacles

▲ This shrimp is hiding from **predators.**

An anemone stings **prey** with its tentacles to make it still. Then it pulls it into its mouth. Some animals use anemones for protection. They hide among the anemone's tentacles.

Sea urchins move using suckers like starfish. They also have spikes that help to push them along. When they find seaweed, they scrape it up and eat it with the teeth under their shell.

▼ A sea urchin's shell is covered with spikes.

▲ This sea urchin has seaweed on its spikes.

The sharp spikes stop some animals from eating sea urchins. Sea urchins also catch stones and seaweed on the spikes that help to **camouflage** them from **predators**.

Tide Pool Tips

All tide pools are different, but most are full of colorful and exciting animals. Sit quietly by a tide pool and watch carefully. What can you see?

▼ Many tide pools are bursting with life!

▲ It is important to stay safe while you explore.

Have fun at tide pools, but remember:
- Be careful what you touch, because some animals can sting or nip.
- Only remove empty shells from the water.
- Be careful when walking over slippery rocks on the **seashore**.
- Watch out for waves and rising seawater.

Glossary

antennae (singular: antenna) thin parts on the heads of some animals, including beetles and lobsters, that are used to feel and touch

camouflage cover or disguise that helps something blend in with its background and makes it hard to see

digest change food into substances that an animal's body can use for energy and to stay healthy

egg object produced by a female animal that can develop into or contain a growing young animal

female sex of an animal or plant that is able to produce eggs or seeds. Males are the opposite sex.

habitat place where particular types of living things are likely to live. For example, polar bears live in snowy habitats and camels live in desert habitats.

hatch come out of an egg

male sex of an animal or plant that is unable to produce eggs or seeds. Females are the opposite sex.

pincer body part made of two movable, sharp pieces that can grasp things

predator animal that hunts and catches other animals for food

prey animal that is caught and eaten by another animal

seabird type of bird that normally lives by the sea, such as gulls or oystercatchers

seashore land at the edge of the sea or ocean that is usually rocky or sandy

shelter place that provides protection from danger or bad weather

tentacle long, thin body part of some animals, used to feel around them so they can find or capture food

Find Out More

Books

Parker, Steve. *Seashore* (Eyewitness). New York: Dorling Kindersley, 2004.

Spilsbury, Louise. *Coastal Treasure Hunter* (Crabtree Connections). New York: Crabtree, 2011.

Woodward, John. *Along the Shore* (Oceans Alive!). Redding, Conn.: Brown Bear, 2009.

Web sites

Facthound offers a safe, fun way to find web sites related to this book. All of the sites on Facthound have been researched by our staff.

Here's all you do:

Visit www.facthound.com

Type in this code: 9781432971977

Index